WINNING IN BASEBALL

Everything You Need
to Succeed on the Diamond

SKY BENSON

TABLE OF CONTENTS

CHAPTER 1

THE SCIENCE OF HITTING

Pitch Recognition

"Fastballs, Curves, and Changeups"

Imagine yourself in the batter's box, heart palpitating, facing a pitcher capable of hitting a pitch 95 mph. The game is tied with two outs in the bottom of the ninth inning. Everything depends on how you swing it next. Pitch recognition, however, is the covert tool that has the power to change the game. Pitch identification, to put it simply, is the capacity to identify the type of pitch that the pitcher is throwing before it reaches the plate. It's akin to possessing a sixth sense, an ability that sets exceptional players apart. The benefits include increased confidence at the plate, improved timing on your swings, and more contact. However, mastery requires effort, patience, and an acute eye for detail. Now, let's break down the most pitches you'll face: the changeup, curveball, and fastball.

The Speed King: Recognizing the Fastball

It is the pitching world's most dominant weapon, with average fastball velocity ranging from 85 to 100 mph. Imagine a blur streaking in your direction; it is the hallmark move of the fastball. It may seem to "tunnel" at you because of its minimal movement—a direct shot from the pitcher's hand to your bat.

Another hint is to pay attention to the distinctive "crack" sound that appears at impact. The sound of a bat striking a fastball squarely is a gratifying symphony. The problem is that even while the pace is frightening, it is also predictable. A fastball is an untick-loving fastball. You stand a higher chance of squaring it up for a good hit if you can identify it early.

A Trick Drop: Identifying the Curveball

The curveball throws a curveball instead of the fastball's simple approach (pun intended). This pitch's distinct spin allows for a dramatic downward bend. Curveball operates similarly to a magician pulling a rabbit out of a hat. It could appear like a tasty fastball when it begins its voyage high in the strike zone, but it could quickly plummet and leave you flailing. Here's how to recognize the cunning of the curveball: Keep an eye out for the ball to appear to "dive" or "drop" as it gets closer to the plate. It could seem to levitate momentarily before defying gravity. A further red flag is the spin. Compared to fastballs, curveballs frequently have a more apparent rotation. Sometimes, hitters with experience can detect this slight difference. Recall that a curveball travels slower than a fastball, usually between 70 and 80 mph. You should modify your swing and prepare for the drop if it appears to "hang" in the air for an extra beat.

The Master Pretender: Recognizing the Shift

The ultimate master of disguise is the changeup. Pitchers toss it differently than they would a fastball, giving the impression that it is slower and misleading hitters. Envision a fastball that abruptly breaks in midair. That's the hidden weapon of the changeup. Pay attention to the ball's path.

In contrast to a fastball, does it appear to "hesitate" or even "slow down" as it approaches the plate? The sound is another hint. Upon contact, a changeup's "thud" sound is usually duller than a fastball's "crack." Batters with experience may notice a difference since a changeup hits the bat with less force than a fastball. Recall that the entire strategy of the changeup is based on deceit. Its slower speed fools you into thinking it's a fastball, then knocks you off balance. You can prevent swinging too early and be prepared to establish firm contact by being aware of the slight variations.

Refining Your Craft: The Way to Expert Pitch Recognition

Gaining pitch recognition skills is a process rather than a final goal. It requires patience, commitment, and a readiness to grow from your errors. Experience gained in the real world cannot be replaced. Practice batting against a pitching machine or other pitches thrown by teammates. Your eyes will get better at telling apart different speeds and spin the more you see them. Examine your at-bat replays. Concentrate on the pitches you thought you knew, then examine what went wrong. Were you blind to a visual cue? Did you misinterpret the pitcher's arm action? Making improvements requires learning from your failures. Power comes from knowledge. Do some homework on the pitchers you will be facing before you take the field. Examine game film, study their pitching habits, and look for distinguishing features in delivering fastballs, curveballs, or changeups. You can get a significant edge by being aware of what to anticipate.

Above and Beyond: Sophisticated Methods for Pitch Identification

While grasping the basics is essential, there's always more to learn. Skilled batters occasionally can read the pitcher's body language and deduce subtle hints. Does a curveball cause their windup to shift slightly? Do they walk differently when they switch things up? These minute variations have the power to alter everything. Count the changeups, curveballs, and fastballs thrown during the at-bat. This enables you to anticipate what will happen next. To keep you off balance, a pitcher who has mainly thrown fastballs may be about to deliver a changeup. Though it's only a game of chance, remember that it can be a helpful tool. You may occasionally hear the catcher signaling for a particular pitch. Even though it's not always accurate, this can offer beneficial information, mainly if the catcher and pitcher aren't communicating well.

Embrace Your Gut Feelings

Pitch recognition development involves more than simply visual and mechanical analysis. It also has to do with developing an affinity for the game. A skilled batter may occasionally "feel" a particular pitch coming, even if they aren't aware of every little aspect. Have faith in your intuition, and don't hesitate to modify your strategy in response to your gut.

The Skill of Waiting

You can't learn to recognize pitches by hitting at everyone. It all comes down to waiting for the ideal pitch to land. You may make the pitcher work around you by being patient at the plate and knowing the different pitches. You'll see more pitches, take more walks, and eventually be better positioned to drive the ball hard when the pitch is in your favor.

The quest for pitch recognition lasts a lifetime. You'll run against different pitchers with fresh pitches on your baseball adventure. Take on the challenge, never stop learning, and believe in your skills. You'll go from being a passive hitter to a master of the plate with commitment and practice, using pitch awareness as your covert weapon.

Mastering Batting Mechanics

"Balance, Stance, and Swing Technique"

Imagine hitting a pitch so hard that it goes over the outfield wall and into the stands for a home run. A symphony of power and accuracy, it's a feeling like no other. But it would help if you had more than raw strength to do this magic at the plate. It all comes down to good batting techniques, which are the building blocks of a good swing. Think of the way you hit the ball as a well-oiled machine. Your position, balance, and swing technique must work together perfectly to get power and bat speed. Here is a detailed look at the most important things that will help you go from being a nervous hitter to a confident slugger.

Finding Your Center: Why Stance Is Important

Everything that happens in your swing starts with your attitude. Your body tells you, "I'm ready to hit the ball hard!" A balanced stance gives you a stable base for building power and lets you respond quickly to any ball. Keep your feet shoulder-width apart to build a strong base. One foot can be slightly pushed forward to stabilize the body and help the power flow. Try different things until you find what fits you best and let your weight rest evenly. Keep your knees slightly bent so they are ready to use energy in your swing. This also allows quick changes based on where the ball is. Keep your back straight and your core tight. Do not slouch because it lowers your power and makes it harder to hit the ball. Think of a strong string pulling you up straight from your chest. Keep your hands close to your body and hold the bat easily with a loose grip. This gives you more control and lets you hit the ball faster through the hitting zone.

The Art of Balance: How to Stay Stable During the Swing

Balance is the hidden hero of how to bat. It makes your swing less stable, reducing your speed and accuracy. Start your swing by moving your weight from your back to your front foot. Instead of lunging forward, think of it as moving your weight from one leg to the other. The moment you hit the ball, don't stop. Rotate your hips and follow through with your whole body to finish your swing. This keeps your balance and ensures you put all your power into the ball.

The Science of the Swing: How to Get Power and Contact

Now comes the critical part: the swing itself. Now is the time to gather your strength before you start your swing. Your hands may drop a little, and your weight may move back. It's like winding up a spring before letting go. Your front foot might move forward a little as you start to swing. This helps you move forward and pass power from your legs. Your hips power your swing. Think of your belly button moving toward the pitcher as you turn your hips. This strong move moves power from your core to your upper body and then to the bat. This refers to your bat's direction as it swings through the hitting zone. A level swing line is ideal because it lets you hit the ball consistently hard. The exact moment your bat strikes the ball is the goal of hitting. If you want the most strength and line drives, hit the ball just before the front plate.

Getting better at hitting the ball: "Practice Makes Perfect"

Getting good at hitting takes time, hard work, and a lot of practice. Work on your swing technique without a ball. You can then focus on your form and muscle memory. Hitting off a tee is a great way to focus on specific movements, such as the bat path and the point of contact. For the front toss, have someone throw you softballs so you can focus on the timing and touch without worrying about a pitcher throwing fastballs. Record yourself hitting and look at the video. Watch your stance, balance, and the direction of your swing. Find places where you can do better and make the necessary changes. Don't be afraid to get comments on your mechanics from a coach or more experienced player. There isn't a single way to hit the ball that works for everyone. People with different body types and dancing styles can do well. Balance, power transfer, and a smooth swing path are the most important things to remember as you find what works best for you.

More Than Just the Basics: Advanced Batting Techniques

Learning the basics is a good start, but there's always more to learn about how to hit the ball. There are different kinds of pitches. Making small changes to your technique for fastballs, curveballs, and changeups is very important. To hit line drives off of fastballs, keep your swing path flat. If the pitcher throws a curveball, you might need to slightly move your swing line up to account for the ball rolling down. When you get a changeup, you should expect the pitch to be slower, so change the speed of your bat to match. It's tough when you only have two strikes left. This is the most crucial time to shorten your swing and focus on making good contact. By moving your hands closer to the knob and "choking up" on the bat a little. You can make the bat go faster and improve your chances of getting the ball in play. Don't follow the rules. Power-hitting is fun, but if you can hit the ball to all areas, pitchers will have a terrible time stopping you. Use the whole field to your advantage and practice hitting line shots to the other field. Bat speed is an essential part of hitting hard. To safely and successfully increase your bat speed, you can do different exercises and drills as part of your training. Focus on strengthening your core, shoulders, and legs through exercises, as these muscles significantly make your bat speed.

Strength and conditioning are the most critical parts of mechanics.

How you hit the ball is fundamental, but it's not the only thing that matters. You can move power from your lower body to your upper body and stay stable during your swing if you have a strong core. Planks, sit-ups, and Russian twists are all exercises that can help you build core power. Power is made possible by solid legs. Jumping exercises like squats, lunges, and plyometrics can help you get more powerful and move power from your legs to your core and swing. It would help if you had strong shoulders to handle the bat and make it go faster. Rows, external rotations, and internal rotations are some exercises that can help strengthen your shoulders and keep your rotator cuff healthy.

Building Mental Toughness: How to Stay Sharp at the Plate

Physical strength and how you hit the ball are essential but don't forget how important mental toughness is. Picture yourself hitting the ball hard. Picture yourself hitting the ball hard and sending it where you want it. Visualization can help you concentrate and feel more confident at the plate. Don't let the result stress you out. Pay attention to every part of your swing, from start to end. Trust your skills and keep an open mind as you go into each pitch. Everyone gets hit by a pitch. Keep your mistakes in the past. Change how you do things based on what they taught you and stay upbeat at the plate. A good attitude can have a significant effect on how well you do.

To become a master hitter, you must work at it long. As you get better at baseball, you'll encounter different pitching types and game conditions. It would help if you were always willing to learn and improve your skills. The best batters are always looking for ways to get better. Take on the task, stick with your practice, and enjoy the process of making your swing stronger and more consistent. If you work hard and get the right help, you can go from being a nervous batter to a devastating force at the plate.

Developing a Hitting Approach

"Situational Hitting and Exploiting Pitching Patterns"

The game is tied at the bottom of the ninth, and you have a crucial at-bat. There are two outs, and the bases are total. Even though things are tough, you're staying cool. Why? Why? Because you have a plan—a straightforward way to hit that considers the situation and the pitcher's style. There's more to developing a hitting approach than just trying to hit the ball hard. It's about learning to hit strategically, changing based on the game, and taking advantage of the pitcher's flaws. You can go from being a reactive batter to a master planner with a bat in your hand by following these steps.

Know Yourself and Your Strengths

Being aware of yourself is the basis of any good hitting strategy. Do you hit for power and love fastballs, or do you hit for contact and want to get the ball in play? It is imperative to know your skills and weaknesses. If you have much natural power, get good pitches to hit and let your swing go. In your hitting zone, look for fastballs and change how you hit breaking balls. No matter the pitch, your main goal should be to make steady contact. Learn to hit the ball in all areas and have a wide strike zone. Use hit-and-run or look-to-take pitches when runners are on base to draw walks and make the pitcher work around you if your speed is vital.

Situational Hitting: How to Think Like a Chess Master

There are different ways to play baseball; your approach to the plate should change based on those scenarios. Focus on making good contact and getting the ball into play early on. You can help your team get going and possibly set up chances to score later in the game. "Scoring Position" means a runner is on second or third base. When this happens, your main goal is to drive them in. If you see a pitch you can handle, change your swing to hit a line drive or ground ball that can score a runner. When you have two outs, the pressure builds. You can still try to hit the ball into play, but you might want to shorten your swing and focus on making contact instead of strength. A run can still be scored with a well-placed ground ball. The player has the best chance to score when the bases are loaded. Walks are your friend here. Wait your turn and make the bowler work around you. Throw strikes only when they're in the strike zone and be ready to jump on a good pitch to score many runs.

Taking advantage of the other team: recognizing pitching patterns

Each pitcher has their tricks. Some throw fastballs all the time, while others love to mix in curveballs and changeups. You can get a significant edge in the batter's box by studying your opponents and figuring out what they like to do. Look at scouting reports or game footage before meeting a pitcher. Check to see if their pitching style has any trends. For example, do they tend to throw fastballs early in the count? Do they love to throw a curveball when there are already two strikes? It's better to be ready when you know more. Watching your friends at the plate can help you determine how a pitcher throws. Was the batter before you tricked by a curveball? As the count went down, did the pitcher throw a lot of changeups? Keep an eye on what's happening in the field and change how you do things based on what you see.

Putting on your "game face": Keeping your mind focused.

It's not enough to have a good plan. For your hitting strategy to work, you need to be mentally focused. Turn off noises from the crowd and only listen to the thrower and the ball. Think about where you want the ball to go when you hit it. In baseball, there will be times when you feel under a lot of stress. Do not feel too much. Trust what you've learned and follow your plan. Make mistakes and learn from them. Everyone gets hit by a pitch. Keep your mistakes in the past. Think about what went wrong, change how you do things for the next pitch, and keep an upbeat attitude.

The Art of the Hit

Getting better at hitting is an ongoing process. Try different things until you find what works best for you, and always be ready for new scenarios and pitchers. Don't forget that the best pitchers are always learning new things and getting better at what they do. A good coach can help you figure out how to hit the ball better by looking at your skills and weaknesses. Look into how expert batters play the game. Look at what they do in different settings and change it to fit your skills.

Beyond the Basics: More Advanced Ways to Hit

Knowing the basics is essential, but there's always more to learn about hitting. In this approach, the batter hits the first pitch, and the runner on first base steals the second base on the pitch. It can make the defenders work harder and give you chances to score. If there is a runner on third and less than two outs, the pitcher can hit a fly ball deep enough into the outfield to score the runner. This is called the "sacrifice fly." It gets the hitter out but moves the runner up, which could tie or win the game. The Squeeze Play is used when runners are on first and third base. It is a high-risk, high-reward move. When the pitcher bunts the ball softly toward first base, the first baseman has to throw the ball home quickly. This could take the defense off guard and let the runner from third score. This is where what you know about the pitcher's habits comes in handy. If you know that a pitcher has trouble with fastballs when the count is 3-0, wait until they throw a strike. You might get a walk, putting a runner on base for a mate.

Getting a "Hitter's Eye": Figuring Out the Strike Zone

How you hit depends on how well you can spot pitches in the strike zone. Each hitter's strike zone differs based on their height and stance. When you know your strike zone, you can focus on pitches you can hit instead of striking at pitches you shouldn't. Pay attention to how the player throws. When they throw a curveball, does their arm slot change? Does their pitch tip over in any way? Learn to follow the ball as it leaves the pitcher's hand and figure out where it's going quickly. Stick to your rules. Throws that aren't in the strike zone won't fool you. Pay attention to waiting for your pitch and making a good impact.

To hit well, you need to be physically skilled, mentally focused, and able to think strategically. Building a hitting technique is a process, not a goal. Accept that you are learning, try out different methods, and have faith in your skills. With hard work and practice, you'll go from being a passive hitter to a strategic force at the plate. You'll be ready to beat any player the game throws at you.

CHAPTER 2

THE ART OF DEFENSE

Building a Solid Foundation

"Fielding Drills for Smooth Mechanics and Positioning"

You can do more than just hit home runs in baseball. For a defense to be strong, it needs to be based on good handling. Good fielding techniques and the right place to stand are the keys to making plays and stopping the other team, whether patrolling the outfield or holding down the fort in the infield. This is your plan for building a solid base on the field. It's full of drills that will turn you into a defensive machine.

"The Art of the Glove:" How to Master Fielding

Let's make sure we understand the basics before we start the drills. Your field is like the code of defense; it makes your glovework go smoothly. This is where you start, and it lets you respond quickly to any hit ball. Ensure your knees are slightly bent, your feet are shoulder-width apart, and your weight is even. Your glove should be held easily in front of your body, ready to catch any missiles that come your way. If you want to get to the ball quickly, you need to be able to move your feet quickly. It's important to practice keeping your balance and glove position while moving laterally, backpedaling, and lunging forward. The

Transfer is how you get the ball from your glove to your throwing hand. A quick and smooth shift ensures the throw is faster and more accurate. Keep your eyes on the target as you practice moving the ball smoothly from your glove to your hand. To get runners out, you need to throw hard and accurately. Your arms, legs, and core should help you build strength. Work on a smooth move for the fastest and most accurate throw with a lot of follow-through.

Getting Better: Fielding Drills for All Positions

Ground Ball Fungo is a well-known infield drill. A teacher hits ground balls at different speeds and directions to practice for games. Please pay attention to catching the ball, transferring it smoothly, and throwing it correctly to the correct base. It's like making a double play when you do this drill. Set up bases made of cones and practice fielding ground balls, moving quickly, and throwing across the pitch to make it look like a double play. Place the cones differently and practice moving side to side to catch ground balls hitting your left or right. For those tricky in-between hoppers, this drill helps you better move your feet and react quickly.

Drills for the outfield

Get a partner and have them hit fly balls of different lengths and heights. To keep from running into your friends, practice keeping your eyes on the ball, backpedaling smoothly, and calling for the ball. Find a wall and hit fly balls against it to improve your skills. Pay attention to judging the depth of fly balls, falling softly when you catch them and moving smoothly from catching to throwing them back to the infield. Please set up a target and throw at it from different directions and distances to make it feel like you're going to other bases. This drill helps you get better at throwing and build arm power.

Drills for Everyone

As for cone drills, arrange them in a square or triangle shape and move through them while keeping the proper fielding position. This drill will help you get faster, more agile, and more active overall. Have someone hit you with a line drive from close range. Pay attention to moving quickly, closing your glove to catch the ball, and absorbing the impact. This drill helps you better handle hard-hit balls and coordinate your hands and eyes. Find a partner and throw the ball back and forth with them. Work on being accurate and getting farther each time. This drill helps you get more muscular arms and learn to throw better. Consistency is important. These drills will help you get much better at catching if you do them regularly. Start slowly and focus on good form over speed. As you get better, slowly make the moves harder.

Beyond the Drills: Setting Yourself Up for Success

It's not enough to catch the ball; you must be in the right place at the right time. Each player is responsible for a particular area. Learn the defensive alignments for your role and know where you should be before each pitch. Talk to your teammates! Tell them where you're playing and ask for fly balls to keep people from running into each other. For a defense to work well, there must be clear communication. Your protective alignment may change slightly depending on the batter's stance and how hard they hit the ball. Be aware of these changes and change where you're standing to match.

Building a Team Wall: Fielding Drills to Bring People Together and Improve Communication

Even though each player's skills are essential, catching is a team sport. Every player on a good defense works together to stop the other team, like a well-oiled machine.

Group Work Drills

For this drill, two coaches or partners must hit fungus at the same time. There are multiple balls in play simultaneously, making it feel like a real game and forcing players to talk to each other and work together to catch and field the balls neatly. Set up stations that look like different bases and have players throw the ball around the "diamond" to fake relay throws from the outfield to the infield and from the infield to home to tag runners. This drill is about talking to each other, being accurate, and getting into a rhythm when moving from one place to another. Make practice more like a game. Let's say there are two runners on first and second, and a ground ball is hit to shortstop. Run these drills as fast as the game would, so players must respond quickly, talk about throws, and run plays as a team.

It's essential to communicate.

The glue that ties a defense together is clear and direct communication. Outfielders should clearly and loudly call for fly balls to avoid misunderstandings and collisions. Say simple things like "I got it!" or "Mine!" Infielders backing up throws must let the other fielders know they are there. A simple "on you" or "backing up" can keep you from making mistakes and give you a safety net for throws that go a little off target. Depending on how the batter usually hits the ball, infielders may move before each pitch. Make sure everyone knows about these changes and is in the right place.

Putting together a good attitude

The act of fielding can be difficult. A good mood spreads like wildfire. Honor good plays and cheer people on when they make a mistake. Remember that everyone makes mistakes; what counts is how you handle them. Go over defense mistakes after practice and have a debriefing. As a team, learn from your mistakes and work on how you talk to each other and do things better in those situations. Have fun as you learn and get better together. A fun and happy practice space helps people work together and talk to each other better on the field.

Building a solid defense takes time, hard work, and regular practice. Follow the drills mentioned above and communication tips. You'll see your team go from being a group of individuals to a cohesive defensive unit ready to stop any attack that comes their way. You can build a wall without holes in it if you work together.

Mastering Your Position

"Specific Skills for Infielders, Outfielders, and Catchers"

We've discussed how critical good mechanics, stance, and communication are for a strong defense. Now, let's talk more about the specific skills needed for each field job. From being a generalist to a defense expert, you'll become good at your job by learning its details.

"In the Thick of It: Key Skills for Infielders"

The defensive core comprises the infielders, who are constantly moving and in charge of various plays. First basemen must learn how to catch low throws in the dirt work on hitting with two hands while wearing a soft glove for better control. An excellent first baseman should be able to stretch for throws that are just a little off-target. To catch those close throws, work on your balance and flexibility. Baserunners will stay honest if they know you can see them and stop them from stealing bases. Develop a throwing style that makes it hard for runners to take the lead by practicing quick throws. The second baseman is very important for turning double plays. Smooth footwork, fast changes of direction, and strong throws to first base should all be practiced.

Second basemen are often a part of force plays. Get excited about the game and be ready to act quickly when ground balls are hit at you. As long as there are runners on base, the second fielder might have to cover first base. Ensure you can talk to the first baseman and that the shift from hitting to covering the bag goes smoothly. Shortstops need to cover a lot of ground in the infield. Do drills that help you move quickly from side to side to get to ground balls hit from any direction. A lot of the time, shortstops have to catch ground balls while going toward or away from the batter. Practice fielding while moving while keeping your body and hand in the right place. To turn double plays and get runners out, you need to be able to throw across the field firmly and accurately.

Vast Territory: In-Field Mastery

Outfielders need to be able to cover a lot of ground, which means they need skills that are different from those of infielders. Outfielders must be able to judge fly balls and follow their path. Learn how to read the ball's spin, guess where it will go, and talk to your friends to avoid collisions. Outfielders must be good at running routes to fly balls fast. Get better at predicting where the ball will land and taking good shots. It might look easy to catch fly balls, but you have to be able to judge the depth and time your jump perfectly. You can improve your hand-eye balance and learn how to judge fly balls in the air by practicing catching them against a wall. Strong throws from the outfield can stop runners at the plate or baserunners trying to move up. Build your arm strength and learn how to throw so that aim is more important than power.

The Quarterback of the Defense: Catchers Need These Skills

The catcher is in charge of defense on the field and calls throws, sets up pitches for strikes, and blocks pitches in the dirt. Catchers need gloves that are smooth and reliable. It would help if you got used to quickly taking fastballs, breaking balls, and changeups while still using the proper framing technique. Throwing dirt balls to stop wild pitches from going past the backstop keeps the catcher from getting hit. For good blocking, build up your leg and core power. Catchers are very important because they call pitches based on the batter's history and the game's current state. Learn how to order pitches and plan your moves for the game. This is called "throwing out baserunners." Catchers can stop baserunners who are trying to steal bases. Learn to throw quickly and focus on accuracy when you throw to stop runners. Mastering your position takes hard work and regular practice. Work out with coaches and teammates, and use drills that are made for your role. Constantly improve at what you do well and fix what you need to work on.

"Beyond the Basics: Advanced Skills for Every Job"

Use different pivot steps and throws to work on your advanced double-play moves. Improve your barehanded plays for cuts or bunts that get past the glove. Get better at spotting bunts and quickly suffocating them. Outfielders, get better at reading a batter's swing and guessing what kind of contact will happen (fly ball, line drive, ground ball) so you can take better routes. Do conversation drills with the other outfielders to ensure changes and fly ball calls go smoothly. Improve your pitch-framing skills to make pitches that are close to being strikes look like they are strikes. Learn how to frame fastballs, breaking balls, and off-speed pitches differently. To keep a player focused during the game or calm them down after a rough inning, you should learn how to deal with them during the game.

The Journey That Never Ends

It takes time and practice to get good at your defense position. The battle will get more challenging as you get better at baseball. Please pay attention to how professional athletes who play their roles handle different situations. Look at their strategies and add parts that work for how you play. Take a video of yourself doing drills or playing games. Review the video and find places where you can do better. This kind of self-analysis can help you find your weaknesses and keep track of your growth. Being smart is essential for defense. Keep calm and follow your gut on the field when things get tough. Visualize yourself making plays and staying upbeat during the whole game.

You can make your defense a force to be reckoned with by improving your skills and encouraging good communication within your team. The defense is the most crucial part of any baseball team. Take pride in how good you are at defense, enjoy the task of getting good at your position, and watch as your squad shuts down offenses and wins one play at a time.

Base Running Smarts

"Strategy, Speed Drills, and Stealing Bases Effectively"

There's more to baseball than just home runs and strikeouts. It is a strategy game where every move on the basepaths can change the result. Now is the time to be smart about running the bases. Heads-up baserunners can make scoring more straightforward for the other team, pressure the defenders, and even steal a base or two. Now that you know how to run bases, you can become a base-stealing monster (in a good way, of course!).

How to Think Like a Chess Master: Base Running Strategy

Before we start the drills, let's discuss the strategy side of base running. Are you a fast runner who loves to steal bases? Or maybe a potent bat who focuses on getting on base to score? How you move on the basepaths depends on what you know about your skills and weaknesses. A smart baserunner watches how the pitcher throws. How slowly does the bowler throw? A long windup? Figuring out these patterns can give you a significant edge when stealing something. The best way to run bases changes depending on the game. In the early innings, you might need to move forward on contact to put pressure on the defenders. You might need to be more careful in the late innings to keep the lead. Taking bases is an exciting strategy, but it must be carefully thought through. Before you try to steal, look at the score, the pitcher's arm strength, and the catcher's catching skills. A good steal at the right time can sometimes change the course of the game, but a lousy steal can lead to a crucial out.

Speed drills for base runners as part of "Building Your Engine."

It would help if you were fast on the basepaths, but it's not the most important thing. Do full-out short sprints (30–40 yards) to work on your powerful starts. This gives your legs the strength and speed they need for short basepath runs. These exercises help your legs move faster and work together better. Keep your running form straight by bringing your knees up and kicking your heels towards your hips. Practice quick starts from the lead position to get a feel for what it's like to jump on a steal try. Pay attention to using your strength to push off the front foot and drive into your lead. You must learn how to slide if you want to dodge tags and stay safe on the basepaths. Focus on keeping your body low to the ground and extending your lead leg as you practice moving the right way.

The Art of the Steal: Tacks and Strategies

Stealing bases is exciting, but you must be very careful with your timing and performance. A good lead gives you an edge when you try to steal. Get good at taking a safe lead that lets you respond quickly to the pitcher's throw. In this case, you start with a more significant lead and then cut it down right before the bowler throws. This makes it hard for the catcher to keep up, which opens the door for a successful steal. Someone good at running bases can read and tell the pitcher's body language. A slight hitch in the throw or a look to first base could mean someone is trying to steal, so you must get back to the bag. Stealing bases is a play with a lot of risk and gain. Don't take chances; only try to steal if the case calls for it, and you can succeed.

Beyond Speed: Getting Smarter at Baserunning

Base running is more than being fast, even though speed is essential. Good baserunners know what will happen before it does. To avoid running into your friends, learn how to tag up on fly balls, when to round first on a line drive, and how to run the bases properly. Knowing when to take extra bases and when to hold can be very important, depending on the game. Consider what's happening, talk to your coach, and make intelligent basic choices. Keep an eye on the basepaths at all times. Watch for chances to move forward on wild pitches, passed balls, or mistakes made by the defense. Taking advantage of these mistakes can lead to scoring chances.

The Art of the Slide

Baserunners need to be able to slide to avoid being tagged and get to the base safely. Slide right before you get to the bottom. This cuts down on the distance you have to slide and lets you get back on your feet faster if needed. Ensure your lead leg is in front of you, your body is low to the ground, and you wear safety gear like sliding pads. This is the most popular slide, and it's used to come up to a base head-first. Hitch your inside leg around the base to stay in touch with the bag. The feet-first slide is used when going up to a base with your feet first. It's usually done to avoid hitting the catcher. For safety, tuck your chin in and keep your arms tucked in.

How to Stay Safe

Baserunning can be dangerous, but safety is the most important thing. Know Your Limits" means don't push yourself further than your body can handle. If you're tired or hurt, it might be best to skip a steal try. Always let your coach know what you want to do before you try to steal. They will look at the game conditions and give you advice based on that. Stretching and training the right way is crucial to keep from getting hurt on the basepaths.

Don't be a bother, but be a good bother.

An innovative and bold baserunner can make things complicated for the other team. They throw off the pitcher's rhythm, keep the defenders on their toes, and make it possible for runs to score. Always make it seem like you might steal. This stresses the pitcher and catcher and could give your friends chances at the plate. Come up with unique ways to move forward on the basepaths. Using fake leads, delayed steals, and defense mistakes to your advantage is possible. Stay focused on the game the whole time. One error in judgment on the basepaths can lead to an expensive out.

Becoming good at running to bases takes time, hard work, and a mix of mental and physical skills. Practice often, learn as much as you can about baseball, and always try to be a threat on the basepaths. You can become a valuable addition to your team by combining speed and smarts. You can steal bases and make things difficult for the other team. Prepare to be a baserunning threat (but a safe and responsible one!) by putting on your cleats and training your reflexes.

CHAPTER 3

MASTERING THE MENTAL GAME

"A Team Approach"

Building a Fortress of Focus

Baseball is both a physical and mental race. Focusing under pressure, avoiding distractions, and keeping calm are all critical for the success of a team. To make a "fortress of focus" with your partner, do the following:

Improving Your Group's Focus

Set up routines before the game that will help you stay focused and calm. This could be done through group meditation, visualization techniques, or just saying positive affirmations over and over again. Distractions and noises outside can make it hard to concentrate. Talk about ways to keep each other from getting distracted as a team, such as telling each other to stay in the present and block out background noise. Clear conversation helps people remain calm. Set up a way to communicate about defensive shifts, pitch types, or base running plays through hand gestures or short verbal cues. This makes things more transparent and helps everyone stay focused on their jobs.

How Positive Affirmations Can Help You

Make short, positive statements that everyone on the team says together before the game or when things get tough. Some examples of mantras are "We got this!" and "Focus on the next pitch." Repeating them makes us more likely to believe in each other and have a winning attitude. Celebrate wins, no matter how big or small. A partner dives to make a catch? Have a party! Does a great play on defense get out? Give each other a high five! Everyone is motivated to keep doing their best work because positive feedback keeps the energy high. As a way to encourage one another, Things go wrong. Build an environment of support instead of focusing on them. A friend hits a home run? Say nice things about them and remind them of their skills. This creates a good team atmosphere where everyone feels like they can get back on track after a failure.

Your team goes from being a group of people to a cohesive unit by working together to build a fortress of focus. You'll be better able to deal with stress, keep distractions to a minimum, and keep your cool during every play. Always keep in mind that a team that works together wins.

Learning from Mistakes Collectively

Baseball is a game where you can learn. Strikeouts, mistakes, and tough losses are all going to happen. However, how these failures are dealt with is what makes a good team great. Here's how to create a "collective learning" mindset where mistakes are seen as chances to learn and grow:

Open communication is key

Make sure players can admit when they're wrong without worrying about being judged. Allow friends to talk about what went wrong and how they can do better after making a mistake. It's not helpful to think about who made the mistake. Instead, think about how to solve the problem. As a group, you should look at what happened, figure out what went wrong, and come up with ways to avoid making the same mistakes again. Everyone messes up and can learn something from it. Get your friends to talk about their thoughts and experiences. Every member of the team can do better if they learn from each other's mistakes.

Analysis of the Team for Growth

Watch mistakes and missed plays on video to look at them as a team. This lets people see how things are going from a different angle and figure out what they can do better. "Role-playing scenarios" is a safe way to practice dealing with challenging scenarios. Play out possible mistakes, like passing the ball or missing a throw, and work as a team to come up with good answers. Recognize and praise efforts to get better, not just perfect plays. After a wild ball, did a player work on how they throw? Appreciate how hard they've worked! This good feedback encourages people to keep learning and growing.

When you adopt a "collective learning" mindset, mistakes stop being reasons to give up and start being valuable lessons. The team will learn how to solve problems, gain trust through open conversation, and become more assertive on the field as a whole. The best teams move on from their mistakes after they happen. So, see failures as opportunities to grow and watch your team reach new heights!

CHAPTER 4

UTILIZING YOUR BENCH

"Strength in Numbers"

The Bench

"A Wellspring of Support"

People who start the game usually get the most attention in baseball. But those nine players aren't the only ones who make up a winning team. The unsung stars on the bench are significant to the success of a team. Here's why having a solid bench is helpful and how to make sure those players are always ready to help:

Strength in Numbers: Why a Deep Bench Is Important

Think about a starting pitcher who is getting tired in the late innings. Or a key player getting hurt and needing a defensive backup. A deep bench makes sure that you have skilled players ready to take over right away, keeping the momentum going and giving you strategic benefits. A good bench has players who can hit for power, average, or situational hitting, like a pinch hitter who does well against certain pitchers. This lets you change your attack plan depending on how the game is going. Some players on the bench are great at certain defensive spots. If you have a defensive replacement ready, you can take advantage of holes in the other team's lineup or fix any defensive problems your stars may be having.

Holding the bench in place: ready to go when called upon

Your team will lose if your bench isn't involved. Help bench players feel like they fit and are part of a group. Tell them to stay involved in the game by supporting and cheering on their friends. Schedule scrimmages or intra-squad games so that players on the bench can show off their skills and stay sharp while the leaders get most of the playing time. Sessions that are specifically designed to help bench players improve skills they can use in the game. This could be base-running drills for a spot runner or hitting practice for someone who might come in late in the game.

You can get a hidden edge if you know how vital a strong bench is and use strategies to keep them interested. Your bench players don't just sit there and do nothing; they become a source of support, ready to step up when needed and eventually lead your team to victory. It can make the difference between winning and losing close games to have a strong bench full of determined players.

Pinch Hitting for Success

Late in the game. A critical hit with the game on the line. Right now is the time for the pinch hitter to shine. Who does the call go to? It's not enough to just put any guy up to bat. Choosing the right pinch hitter is like making an intelligent move in chess that can help you score more runs. How to go about "pinch-hitting for success":

Matching up for the most impact

Teams usually send a left-handed batter up against a right-handed pitcher (or the other way around) because the batter has a better view of the pitcher. This makes it easier for the batter to find the point where the ball will be released. When it comes to certain pitchers, each player has strengths and flaws. Look at research reports and past performance records to find a pinch hitter who has done well against the other pitcher in the past. No matter what hand a player is using, they might be on a hot run at times. Situational specialists, on the other hand, who have a history of doing well in specific scenarios (like with runners in scoring positions), can be beneficial as pinch-hitters.

Making the Most of the Chance to Pinch Hit

Most of the time, pinch players don't have as much time to warm up as starting batters. Pay attention to drills that are like real games, like recognizing fastballs or specific pitch patterns. Putting yourself in a high-pressure situation takes mental toughness. When they come in as a pinch hitter, players need to be calm, focused, and sure of their skills. Visualization exercises can help them get ready for the task in their minds. A good pinch hitter needs to know exactly what's going on in the game. They can change their strategy based on the score, the number of outs, and the number of runners on base. For example, with runners on base, they might go for a base hit, while with no outs, they might focus on a power swing.

You can turn a possible out into a strategic benefit by carefully choosing a pinch hitter based on matchups and the situation. Putting together a team of "pinch-hitting specialists" who are great in certain situations gives you a lot of offensive options and makes it more likely that you'll win close games. A pinch hit at the right time can be the difference-maker that wins the game for your team.

Matchup Magic

"Defensive Replacements"

Baseball is like chess; the best moves don't always happen until the very end. Managers love defensive subs because they let them change how they line up defensively depending on the other team's lineup and what's happening on the field. To use "matchup magic" with defensive subs, do the following:

Taking advantage of the lineup's flaws

Look at spy reports to find holes in the lineup of the other team. Is a batter known for always pulling the ball? If you move your defense to move the infield closer to the pull side, you may have a better chance of getting a ground out. Some players have trouble with pitchers who throw with the opposite hand. To make it harder for the batter to throw, you might want to move a defender to the other side of the field with a better arm. Your defensive approach may change depending on how many runners are on base and outs there are. When there are runners on base, a team might put more emphasis on a better infield defense to stop stolen bases or ground ball outs that move runners up.

Getting the most out of defensive matchups

Some players have a more extended range, but they may make more mistakes. An excellent fielding defender might be a better choice if the other team has a heavy hitter who hits ground balls. A player with great range in the center is more useful when facing a fly-ball hitter. Make sure that all players know who will play defense instead of them. This makes sure that everyone knows what their new roles and tasks are, which keeps things clear and makes the strategic switch work better. Having players who can play more than one spot gives you more options for defensive replacements. This means that coaches can change their alignment depending on the game without weakening the defense as a whole.

You can use defensive subs very effectively if you know how players tend to play, make the most of defensive matchups, and use players who can do a lot of different things. Late-game changes that take advantage of a weakness in your opponent's team can mean the difference between a routine play and an out that changes the game. There are times when the best players aren't even starting; they're just waiting for their chance to make "matchup magic" happen on the field.

CHAPTER 5

THE STRATEGIST'S MINDSET

Understanding the Game's Nuances

"Situational Hitting, Defensive Shifts, and Exploiting Opponent Weaknesses"

For the most part, baseball is a great mix of skill and planning. Mastering physical skills is essential, but what sets great players apart is knowing how the game works and changing how you play depending on the situation. To raise your baseball IQ, you need to find and use the game's secret gems:

The Art of Hitting Based on the Situation

There are different kinds of hits. It's exciting to hit a huge home run with the bases loaded, but a well-placed ground ball with runners on can be just as helpful—work on hitting the ball and getting it into play. A rally can start with a well-placed single or an out that moves runners along. It's getting late, and the game is close. The pitcher might try to protect the plate and get walks if the score is tied, or the game is near. Even getting a base on balls puts pressure on the pitcher and gives your friends chances to score. "Runners in Scoring Position" means that there are runners on second or third base, and the goal is to drive them in. Find a pitch you can handle and hit the ball hard, either in the air or on the ground, to get an RBI.

How to Read the Signs for Defensive Shifts

Matchups and getting as many outs as possible are critical in modern baseball. The defense might line up in a way you don't expect, like stacking infielders on one side of the field based on how the batter usually hits. If you're a pull hitter who likes to hit the ball to right field, the defenders might move to the right side. Notice the change and make the necessary changes to your hitting approach. Some pull hitters might try to hit the ball the other way or bunt down the line when space is on the other side of the field. If you're good at hitting the ball to the opposite field, shifting to one side of the field can allow easy base hits the other way.

Taking Advantage of Weaknesses: Scouting and Strategy

Every player, batter or pitcher, has good and bad points. Read scouting reports on batters who are up against you. Find out what they tend to do, like if they have trouble with fastballs or breaking balls. You can use this knowledge to call pitches or change where you are on defense. How the batter stands at the plate, swings, and moves should all be watched. These small clues can help you figure out how they're going about things and maybe even what pitch they're after. If a batter has trouble with a particular ball, throw it to them! Also, if a baserunner is known for being unable to steal, a well-timed pickoff attempt could catch them off guard.

Knowing how to play the game well is like having a secret key. You can go from being a passive player to an active strategist on the field by spotting hitting chances in different situations, adapting to defense shifts, and taking advantage of your opponent's weaknesses. Because you know more about baseball, you can make better decisions, predict what will happen, and eventually help your team win more. When you go to the field next time, pay attention to the game inside the game. You'll make a more significant difference in the field if you learn more.

Scouting Your Opponents

"Analyzing Strengths, Weaknesses, and Identifying Game Plans"

Imagine you knew exactly what questions would be on a test before taking it. That's why a baseball team that has been studied well has an edge. Scouting, or studying your opponents, is crucial for getting ahead in a competition. Here's how to become a great detective and discover your competitors' strengths, flaws, and habits.

This is the Scouting Toolbox

Watching a game isn't the only way to scout. These are made by professional scouts or coaches and describe how a player hits, swings, tends to hit certain pitches, and even their skills and weaknesses in the field. Look at videos of your opponents from recent games. Watch their body language at the plate, how they swing, and how they respond to different pitches and fielding situations. Statistics can give us helpful information. Look at a batter's hitting average against various pitchers, how often they strike out, and how powerful they tend to be (ground ball hitter vs. fly ball hitter). Watch how your opponent acts on the field and approaches their at-bats during the game. Look for hints in their body language or how they usually plan things to help you figure out how they think.

How to Figure Out Hitter Tendencies

A batter might hate your fastball more than anything else. Watch the batter's stance, bat speed, and swing line to learn their mechanics. What kind of swing do they have? Do they hit the ball straight up or down? This can show whether they like fastballs or breaking balls. Please choose the correct pitches and watch how the batter responds to them. Do they have trouble with breaking balls that go out of the strike zone, or do they go after high fastballs? Knowing these patterns can help you call the correct pitches as a pitcher. As a player, knowing these patterns can help you guess where they might hit the ball. What kinds of settings does the batter use well? Are they bolder when runners are on base, or do they play it safer? Understanding how they act under pressure can help you guess what they'll do next.

Beyond the Plate: Looking for Pitchers

Don't just pay attention to batters. List the pitcher's different pitches. Do they mostly throw a fastball and a slider, or do they also throw a changeup or a curveball sometimes? As a batter, knowing their tools can prepare you for what's coming. Look at how fast the pitcher's fastball is and how well they can control their pitches. What kind of fastball do they throw? Is it high and tight, or do they paint the zone's sides? As a batter, this knowledge lets you change how you approach the plate. When there are two strikes, does the pitcher nibble at the strike zone's edges, or do they dare batters with fastballs down the middle? As a batter, recognizing these trends helps you guess what might happen next and maybe change your swing to account for it.

From Hints to Game Plans

Scouting is more than just gathering facts. Use the scouting report and your notes to devise a unique way to hit each pitcher. This could mean focusing on certain pitches or searching for specific spots in the strike zone. Change how you're positioned defensively based on how the batter usually hits. For instance, if a batter likes to pull the ball and hit it to right field, you might move the infielders to the right side to prepare for their swing. Spy reports can help you choose which pitches to use if you're a pitcher. Include curveballs more often in your arsenal if a batter has trouble with them.

Getting Better at Scouting

The best scouts are constantly picking up new things. Talk to your friends and coaches about what you saw. By sharing information, you can get a complete picture of your opponents. The more games you watch and think about, the better you'll get at finding patterns and trends. Don't forget about things that seem small. Changing a batter's stance or a pitcher's windup could tell you much about their actions.

You go from being a reactive player to a proactive planner when you get good at scouting. You'll be able to guess what your opponent will do next, take advantage of their weaknesses, and help your team win.

Adapting on the Fly

"Making In-Game Adjustments Based on Situations and Strategy"

Baseball is a game where things are constantly changing. Baseball is not like other sports where there are set plays. Instead, players must be flexible and change their plans as the game progresses. Here are some tips on how to think quickly and make significant changes during a game:

Reading the Game

There is a skill called "reading the game" that every player should have. Making contact and getting on base might be the primary goal early in the game. It might change if the score is close in the late innings to protect the plate and get walks. A batter might be bolder when there are no outs and try to drive in runs. A bunt or well-placed ground ball may be the better move if there are two outs and runners are on. Knowing how fast the baserunners are and how often they take bases can change how you approach them. If a fast runner is on first, a well-placed ground ball can put pressure on the defenders and lead to a base being stolen.

Hitters: Changing How You Approach

The report on the pitcher? You should change your swing to focus on fastballs instead of breaking balls if they throw many of them with two strikes. Pay attention to the pitcher's movements. Are they having trouble keeping their cool? Find pitches that people can hit and take advantage of their mistakes. Do they throw their fastball high and tight? To hit the ball the other way, change your position and swing. If you are an experienced player, you can figure out what pitch is coming by reading the catcher's signs. This knowledge can help you change your swing or even call a timeout to throw off the pitcher.

Pitchers: Making Changes on the Mound

It's the pitcher's job to throw off the batters. Watch how the batter stands and how it swings. A more balanced stance could mean they're ready to wait for a particular pitch, while an eager stance could mean they want to swing early. Make the necessary changes to your pitch choice. The number of balls can change your pitching approach and the strikes you throw. If the count is complete, a well-placed fastball might be the best way to get the batter to swing and miss. Did someone hit your fastball hard earlier in the at-bat? To keep the batter wondering, occasionally throw in a changeup or a breaking ball. Did the batter hit your fastball badly? Feel free to throw it again but be ready to change things if the batter starts to guess what you'll do.

Talking to each other is vital.

You can't adapt on the spot by yourself. The pitcher and catcher work together to change the pitching plan based on the batter and the game. The catcher can offer pitches based on what they see and what the pitcher does well. The defensive arrangement could change based on how the batter hits the ball. For a shift to work, the infielders and outfielders must be able to talk to each other.

You become a more critical and valuable player when you learn to change your mind quickly. You'll adapt to how the game goes, take advantage of weaknesses as they appear, and help your team win. Baseball is a game where things are constantly changing. You should be the kind of player who loves change, knows the game inside and out, and can make good choices quickly.

CHAPTER 6

BUILDING A WINNING MENTALITY

Maintaining Focus and Composure

"Staying Sharp Under Pressure and in High-Stakes Situations"

Baseball can be very stressful. A big strikeout, a situation with many runners on base, or a close game in the late innings can test even the best player. But the best players know how to keep relaxed, concentrate, and be in charge. When you feel stressed, take a few slow, deep breaths. This straightforward thing lowers your blood pressure and calms you down so you can think clearly and act quickly. Think about all the time you spent training. Remember to use your skills confidently, knowing you've been practicing for this. Negative thoughts or mistakes from the past will only get in the way of your success. Change them out for good affirmations. As you prepare, tell yourself, "I can do this" or "I'm focused and ready." Before an important event, close your eyes and picture yourself doing well. Picture yourself hitting a big line drive, throwing strikes, or making a great play. This thought practice makes you feel better about yourself and prepares you for success. Keep your attention on the present. Don't overthink about the past or what might happen next. Be present, pay attention to the job, and respond to what's happening around you.

If you stay focused and relaxed, you can go from being a player who gives up under pressure to one who is calm and sure of themselves. You'll be able to make better choices, use your skills more effectively, and finally step up when the game is on the line. Relax, have faith, and show off your baseball Zen!

Developing Mental Toughness

"Overcoming Challenges, Handling Setbacks, and Bouncing Back"

It's not all sunshine and home runs in baseball. Strikeouts, mistakes, and tough losses are all going to happen. A great player doesn't just have the ability; they also have the mental toughness to deal with problems and get back on track after a setback. Baseball is not a sprint; it's a journey. There will be cold and hot spots. Know that problems will arise; see them as chances to learn and improve. Everybody messes up sometimes. They only make you feel bad when you think about them. Instead, look at what you did wrong when you made a mistake and use that information to improve. It's easy to forget things in baseball. If you struck out in the last inning, it shouldn't change how you hit in the next. Let go of the past and start each game or at-bat with a clean slate. Talking badly to yourself is the worst thing you can do. Could you change it to upbeat affirmations? You've already gotten through tough times, so tell yourself you can do it again.

Before a big game, picture yourself doing well. Picture yourself making the plays, hitting the ball hard, and helping your team win. This mental practice boosts your confidence and prepares you for a good result. "Embrace the Challenge" means not to run away from harsh conditions. Think of them as chances to see your skills and mind's strength. Taking on a task boosts your confidence and shows that you have a strong mind.

It takes time to become mentally tough. It takes constant work and a good attitude. You can build mental toughness to overcome problems and become a more helpful player by taking on challenges, learning from your mistakes, and believing in yourself. Setbacks are only brief, and what makes you successful is how well you can recover from them.

The Power of Positive Thinking

"Maintaining Confidence, Motivation, and a Winning Attitude"

You have to think about baseball as well as move your body. Having a good attitude can mean the difference between hitting a home run that wins the game and striking out. Using the power of positive thoughts can help you feel better about yourself, get more motivated, and do better on the field:

Be sure of yourself

Being confident comes from thinking positively. You confidently go into every at-bat or game when you believe in yourself and your skills. When people are sure of themselves, they can make things run more smoothly, respond faster, and be willing to take risks they know will pay off.

Motivation is Important

Having a good mood makes you more motivated. "I can do this" makes you work harder in practice, stay focused during games, and never give up, even when things get tough. You can always push yourself to improve on the field because of this unwavering drive.

Building a Winning Mindset

Baseball is a game of speed. With an upbeat attitude, everyone on the team feels they can win. Celebrating your friends' wins, focusing on the good things about the game, and keeping the faith that you can win, even when you're behind, can create a positive vibe that can help your team get through challenging situations and win.

Thoughts that are good for you

Negative thoughts are evil for you and will lead to bad things. Instead, use positive mantras to feel better about yourself. Say things to yourself repeatedly before a big game, like "I'm focused and ready" or "I trust my skills." These words can help you stop doubting your abilities and believe you can do your best.

How to Visualize Success

Picture yourself doing well. Before the game, close your eyes and picture yourself hitting a line drive, jumping to catch a ball, or striking out the batter. This thought practice makes good things more likely to happen and prepares your mind for success.

Keeping a Positive Attitude After Setbacks

Everybody messes up sometimes. When you have a positive attitude, you can learn from your mistakes and get back up better. Don't overthink about a wrong move or a play you missed. Look at what went wrong, change how you did things, and then look forward to the next chance.

When you believe in positive thoughts, you change from a player held back by self-doubt to a confident competitor. You'll have a winning attitude going into the game, which will motivate your friends and help your team win. On the baseball field, having a good mood is very helpful. Keep your head up and believe in yourself; your game will reach new heights!

Closing Thoughts

This e-book should have given you the information and tips to do well on the baseball field. Don't forget that being a well-rounded player is more than having good physical skills. It's about knowing the little details of the game, being able to change how you play on the spot, and keeping a happy, focused attitude. As you start playing baseball, be ready for obstacles. You can learn from everything, whether it goes well or not. You will learn more about the game and improve if you play, practice, and think about it more. The most important thing is never to forget how much fun the game is. Baseball is all about working together, having fun, and winning. Celebrate wins with your friends, be there for them when things get tough, and always try to improve. You can become an essential part of your team and leave your mark on the baseball field if you work hard, love the game, and follow the advice in this e-book. Get your glove, walk to the field, and start the game!